ISC

An introduction to the global standard for service management

Second edition

ISO/IEC 20000

An introduction to the global standard for service management

Second edition

DAVID CLIFFORD – FSM^{CM}

IT Governance Publishing

Every possible effort has been made to ensure that the information contained in this book is accurate at the time of going to press, and the publisher and the author cannot accept responsibility for any errors or omissions, however caused. No responsibility for loss or damage occasioned to any person acting, or refraining from action, as a result of the material in this publication can be accepted by the publisher or the author.

Apart from any fair dealing for the purposes of research or private study, or criticism or review, as permitted under the Copyright, Designs and Patents Act 1988, this publication may only be reproduced, stored or transmitted, in any form, or by any means, with the prior permission in writing of the publisher or, in the case of reprographic reproduction, in accordance with the terms of licences issued by the Copyright Licensing Agency. Enquiries concerning reproduction outside those terms should be sent to the publisher at the following address:

IT Governance Publishing
IT Governance Limited
Unit 3, Clive Court
Bartholomew's Walk
Cambridgeshire Business Park
Ely
Cambridgeshire
CB7 4EH
United Kingdom

www.itgovernance.co.uk

© David Clifford 2011
The author has asserted the rights of the author under the Copyright, Designs and Patents Act, 1988, to be identified as the author of this work.

First published in the United Kingdom in 2010
by IT Governance Publishing.

ISBN 978-1-84928-314-4

FOREWORD

This book brings a fresh look at service management, and a better understanding of it. The author provides valuable clarity on efficient teamwork and on the necessity for predictive management to properly implement an effective and sustainable service management system.

In today's world, where many books are published on service management, David offers many years of solid experience, presented in a simple, clear and effective way.

I will be using this book for my consultancy, training and coaching of managers and service management consultants.

I hope that this book will give you a holistic view of the essence of ISO/IEC 20000 and will also help you in your day-to-day activities.

Marc Taillefer

Executive Manager, Consultant and Auditor (EXIN & TÜV SÜD Akademie).

Consultant, trainer, coach and lecturer.

Member of many international standard-writing groups, including service as Secretary for the group writing ISO/IEC 20000 standards.

PREFACE

This introduction is intended to be a handy reference tool that contains, in one place, some of the key information that those working with ISO/IEC 20000 (Part 1, Edition 2, 2011) may need. Part 1 of the ISO/IEC 20000 series provides a list of service management requirements that all service providers should aspire to. There are other parts of the series that are briefly discussed in this publication.

It is certification-scheme neutral (i.e. for companies) and qualification-programme neutral (i.e. for individuals).

It is not a substitute for acquiring and reading the standard itself. Every reader of this book is recommended to read the standard, where further guidance and inspiration can be found.

ABOUT THE AUTHOR

David Clifford is recognised as one of the world's leading authorities on ISO/IEC 20000. He is a regular speaker at international events managed by organisations such as the itSMF and EXIN. David is the author of the itSMF International endorsed publication, *Implementing ISO/IEC 20000 – the roadmap*.

He assisted the itSMF in establishing their certification scheme for ISO/IEC 20000, now owned by APMG International, including auditing the auditors on their behalf. He has also been the prime consultant supporting the initiation and development of the EXIN service management qualification programme aligned with ISO/IEC 20000.

His knowledge, experience and contribution to the service management industry have been formally recognised by the award of the highest credential of 'Fellow' within itSMFI's The priSM Institute®. David is also the global vice-president for priSM®.

David has worked in the arena of business, IT applications and ITSM, supporting multi-billion dollar initiatives on a global scale.

He is an Executive Consultant at enterprise-DNA Limited, a global consultancy and training company.

E-mail: *david.clifford@enterprise-DNA.com*

Web: *www.enterprise-DNA.com*

Web: *www.thepriSMinstitute.org*

ACKNOWLEDGEMENTS

The following people have generously given of their own time by reviewing this publication:

Peter Brooks, itSMF, South Africa

Nora Clifford, enterprise-DNA Limited

Ralph Gray, Lucid IT, New Zealand

Geoff Harmer, Maat Consulting, UK

Suzanne van Hove, SED-IT, USA

Felix Osague, Schlumberger IS, UK

Enrico Rapacioli, BT Expedite, UK

Douglas Read, Hong Kong

Sadao Shiota, HP, Japan

Marc Taillefer, Qualiti7, Canada

Bryan Williams, Capita Secure Information System, UK

Robin Yearsley, IT Training Zone, UK.

Copyright in the ISO/IEC 20000 standard is owned by its publishers.

It can be purchased direct from the ISO website or via *www.itgovernance.co.uk/standards.aspx*.

CONTENTS

Introduction 1
Chapter 1: Background 5
   A new edition of Part 1 5
   Why the need to change? 5
   What are the key changes in Edition 2? 6
   Principles of ISO/IEC 20000 6
   Focus on a customer-driven approach 7
   Focus on end-to-end service management 9
   Focus on integrated service management 10
   Focus on continual improvement 13
Chapter 2: Key Stakeholder Bodies 17
   Customers and end-users 17
   Service providers 17
   Suppliers 20
   Certification bodies 21
   Enabling bodies 23
Chapter 3: Qualification Programmes 25
   Positioning of the EXIN ITSM qualifications 25
   BCS qualification 31
   APMGI qualifications 32
Chapter 4: Compliance and Certification 35
   What is compliance? 35
   What is due diligence? 35
   What is certification? 36
   Why certify? 36
   What is the auditor's approach? 36
Chapter 5: Certification Schemes 38
   The APMGI certification scheme 38
   Other certification schemes 38
   How many certificates have been awarded? 39
Chapter 6: Scope of Assessment 41
   Defining a scope statement 41
   The role of existing certifications 44
Chapter 7: Relationship with other Standards 45
   ISO/IEC 27001 45
   ISO/IEC 15504 45

Contents

   ISO9001 45
   Integrated management systems 46
Chapter 8: The Future of ISO/IEC 20000 .... **47**
   Overview of the parts of ISO/IEC 20000 47
Abbreviations Used **49**
ITG Resources **51**

INTRODUCTION

History has shown that, when one starts to talk about international standards, the sound of voices and running feet can be heard, disappearing into the distance. One hears cries of 'more bureaucracy', 'another certificate for the wall', 'poor management systems can get certified', and 'standards are only of benefit when a customer requires its service provider to get certification.'

Thankfully, we sometimes learn from history and reflect this in our current daily lives, by taking positive steps forward. This is the case with ISO/IEC 20000. It provides a mirror for service providers to compare themselves to.

It provides a list of 'must do' requirements for the service management system (SMS) that all service providers should aspire to.

> A **management system** is 'a set of interrelated or interacting elements to establish policy and objectives, and to achieve those objectives.'

It also provides an initial and substantial target that has been set by practitioners based across the globe. It is a process-based standard that ensures that the management system provides a vehicle in which the commitments to customers can be achieved.

It does not provide advice on *how* to do it, but simply a list of what needs to be done.

A complementary approach can be taken where the standard could, in concept, be viewed as a table of contents of the critical elements of the service provider's best practice framework of choice. A typical example of a framework in the business domain is Business Process Framework, formerly eTom® (for telecommunications companies) and, in the IT domain, others include COBIT®, ITIL® and MOF®, to name but a few.

Introduction

So, for example, where ISO/IEC 20000 says 'The service provider shall create, implement and maintain a capacity plan taking into consideration human, technical, information and financial resources', the framework of choice would give guidance on how this can be achieved. Of course, service providers may also use their own best practices to help to deliver service of an acceptable quality to their customers. The good news is that ISO/IEC 20000 is framework neutral.

> **Note**
>
> Service providers quite often start with their framework of choice when improving their SMS. The framework can span thousands of pages and be quite daunting. Why not open a standard first, that lists the most important elements of service management, and then use the framework for supplementary guidance? This approach gives the potential to be simpler, more efficient and more effective in achieving the objectives.

A common misconception about the standard is that service providers should only be interested in it if they wish to achieve certification. This is not the case. It can also be used simply as an internal benchmark for service providers to assess their capabilities, i.e. to *comply* with the standard, but not to *certify* to it.

ISO/IEC 20000's official title is **Information technology – Service management**. Yes, its roots are planted within the IT domain, but the standard can easily be used by any business that provides a managed service to its customers. This publication has intentionally been written in a context applicable to this philosophy.

For example:

- an insurance company that has a call centre handling claims will need to follow specific procedures, similar to an IT service desk incident management process
- a manufacturing company will need to ensure that it has sufficient resources to deliver to its defined targets, similar to an IT capacity management process

Introduction

- an entertainment company will need to ensure that it closely understands the needs of its customers, and is able to gauge the level of satisfaction with the services to date, similar to an IT business relationship management process.

So, ISO/IEC 20000 can be used by IT service providers and non-IT service providers alike. But how is it used?

Customers are specifying that their service providers must align to the requirements of the standard, thereby improving confidence in the management system and service delivery, as the service provider is independently audited by a certification body.

Service providers are using it as a coherent specification of the things that *must* be done, as opposed to analysing everything that *could* be done. In other words, they are initially concentrating on the critical elements of service management in order to build a firm foundation for any future developments, rather than initially wading through an extensive library of best practice guidance.

Tool vendors are aligning their software to the needs of the standard, so that the tool can support certification/compliance.

Certification bodies are validating that the service provider is performing to an acceptable international standard.

Consultancy companies are performing capability assessments on service providers to enable focused advice to be given on any remedial activities required.

Training providers are expanding their courseware portfolio to include qualifications that are based upon one of the most popular standards that has been produced in this arena.

This introduction is, by definition, an overview of the purpose of the standard and its intended use. Further depth is provided throughout this publication, based upon practical, real-life experiences. Additional guidance can be found in

Introduction

complementary publications (see the resources pages at the end of this book).

CHAPTER 1: BACKGROUND

A new edition of Part 1

The new edition of Part 1 of ISO/IEC 20000 has been released (15th April 2011). The standard is now titled "Information technology – Service Management – Part 1: Service management system requirements". It should be noted that a revised edition of Part 2 of the standard is not due for publication until approximately Q2 2012.

Why the need to change?

Edition 1 of the standard is now some six years old and quite simply, the world in which we live is continually changing. New thoughts regarding how service management should, or in the case of this part of the standard, how service management shall, operate have been reflected in Edition 2. During those six years, there have been new releases of best practice publications. Edition 2 of the standard has remained true to the spirit and intent of its forerunners, namely :

- the standard applies to IT Service Management. Do not try to extend it out into all of IT Governance, software maintenance, etc.
- the standard needs to be able to be certified alone or with ISO9000/ISO27001
- alignment with (not based on) ITIL® is key to a large part of the audience for this standard
- the standard should be minimal in its requirements for production of documents
- the standard needs to be applicable to both large and small service providers in the public and private sectors
- it must not be very prescriptive in how to implement the processes, it should stay at the level of what is to be achieved. This allows many best practice frameworks to be used to support ISO/IEC 20000 e.g. ITIL®, COBIT®, Business Process Framework (eTOM®),

1: Background

eSCM-SP® etc
- ensure that integration of processes is retained as a key principle
- information security process requirements are to remain as a consistent subset of ISO/IEC 27001 to ensure harmonisation
- retain the hierarchy of policy, process, procedure
- retain the need to demonstrate management commitment.

What are the key changes in Edition 2?

Edition 2 is a significant update on Edition 1. The key changes can be broadly categorised as :

- additional requirements – c.35%
- requirements with no fundamental change (being more explicit) – c.40%
- requirements that have not been changed – c.25%

The numbering and naming of chapters in the different sections is largely the same.

Principles of ISO/IEC 20000

ISO/IEC 20000 is based upon a number of fundamental principles that must permeate through the service management system.

Focus on a customer-driven approach, reflecting the agreed needs of the business and its customers in the underpinning management system throughout the full life cycle of the services.

Focus on end-to-end service management, ensuring that suppliers and subcontracted suppliers are aware of their scope of work, have key process touch-points defined, and have sufficient knowledge from the service provider to enable them to do their job in a seamless way.

1: Background

Focus on integrated service management, developing and operating a coherent and holistic service management system that is effective in delivering the desired benefits to the customers, avoiding a 'silo-based' mentality (an approach where each function is focused independent of the others).

Focus on continual improvement, recognising that the business and service management environments are constantly changing, with new demands. Continual improvement will realign service provision and will, for example, increase the efficiency of the management system.

Focus on a customer-driven approach

Without customers, service providers would soon be out of business. The competition for customers is increasingly cut-throat, and service provision is much more of a commodity in these times. So how should a service provider differentiate itself? On cost, or time or quality? In reality, a combination of these factors contributes to the overall perception of the service provider.

From a cost point of view, the service provider typically finds it difficult to recoup the initial investment made during the early life of service provision. The ability to maximise the longevity of the customer relationship, and to cross-sell other services, based upon positive customer experiences and needs, is paramount. But how to do this?

ISO/IEC 20000 specifies a series of requirements for service providers in terms of understanding customer needs, agreeing a scope of work, delivering to that scope, and realigning when the customer needs change.

A supply-and-demand model could be used to assist in satisfying these requirements (*see Figure 1*). Initially, the demand side should, of course, be able to articulate its needs through the use of 'solutioneers' who are designing the business enablers, that is, the business services, business processes, financial models and marketing strategies. Their 'solutioneer' counterparts on the supply side would work closely with them, to advise on enablers to achieve the customer-critical success factors and to develop solution designs.

Once the supply-and-demand elements are designed and integrated, the delivery and operation of those services can be fulfilled.

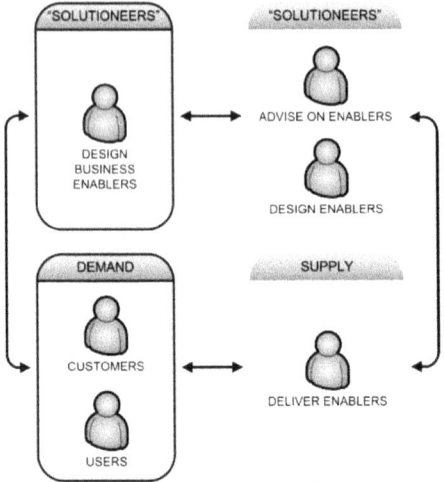

Figure 1: Overview – supply and demand model

Using key performance indicators, cross-referenced to the customer-critical success factors, the delivery link can be maintained. This ensures that the supply side includes performance assessment from a customer perspective as well as an internal perspective. This approach enables an ongoing capability to assess the true value proposition to the customer.

In summary, service providers who align themselves to understanding how their service provision enables the customers to realise benefit will be in a stronger position to differentiate themselves in the market place.

Focus on end-to-end service management

When customers entrust their service provision to a service provider, they expect that the service provider will accept overall accountability for the scope of work. This often includes the management of any suppliers, ensuring a seamless provision of service to the organisation. Figure 2 illustrates this relationship.

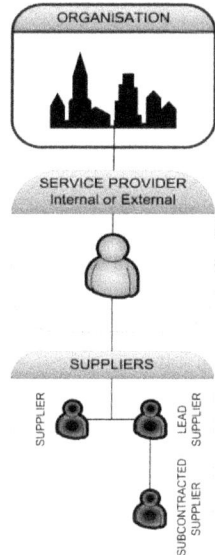

Figure 2: End-to-end relationship model

Service providers may be either internal (the organisation's own staff) or external (a commercial managed service provider) or a combination of both facets. While the implications of service performance may differ between the two, the needs of the service provider are basically the same, in that they need to understand the direction of the organisation and the commitments made to them, and then ensure ongoing service delivery aligned to these needs.

1: Background

It is the responsibility of the service provider to ensure that any outsourced activities are managed so that the commitments are achieved.

It is essential to ensure that the end-to-end relationship model is working well, as one weak link can cause major issues for the organisation. Vertical process integration should, therefore, be a major factor in the design of the management system to support the service life cycle. This will ensure that process touch-points between the service provider and their supply chain are clearly defined.

Timely and accurate information flowing through vertical integration is the lifeblood of a healthy management system. For example, organisation plans regarding new products should be communicated as early as possible to the service provider, who will co-ordinate an assessment of the impact and will design possible solutions. Where applicable, the suppliers will be involved in this assessment at the earliest possible stage.

In summary, treating service design and delivery in a holistic fashion will ensure the existence of a strong supply chain that is ready to meet its commitments as a seemingly single unit.

Focus on integrated service management

It is well documented that a silo-based approach to service delivery will rapidly lead to inefficiencies and an inability to meet the commitments made to the organisation.

When designing or refining the management system, it is important to integrate the processes, not only horizontally, but also vertically, while maintaining focus on the customers/users and building upon the foundation of the SMS general requirements documented in the standard (*see Figure 3*).

1: Background

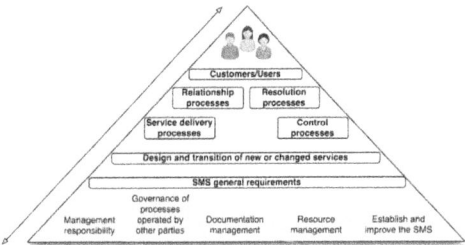

Figure 3: Building on a solid foundation

An iterative approach to SMS design should be employed, based upon initially establishing a firm foundation of objectives, policies and plans.

The *SMS general requirements* (Clause 4 of ISO/IEC 20000) are focused upon this foundation. By defining objectives, policies, plans, process governance, a document management system, an improvement process and, critically, how service provider staff are supported, service provision has a sound starting point. These elements will subsequently influence how the rest of the management system will operate.

Design and transition of new or changed services (Clause 5 of ISO/IEC 20000) is concerned with delivering, changing or retiring services in an effective and consistent way. Once again, the foundation established previously should influence the way in which services are managed through their life cycle.

The other process areas of Figure 3 are summarised below but, again, all of them must align to the initially established foundation.
For example:

- when producing a document such as a Service Level Agreement, it must follow the document management system requirements
- when defining roles, they must align to the structure defined for the competence requirements

1: Background

- when designing processes, the overall service management policy needs to be considered.

Although, for ease of reference, ISO/IEC 20000 categorises processes, it is not intended for service providers to blindly reflect these as functional separators. The content of each category of ISO/IEC 20000 is explained below.

Service delivery processes (Clause 6) includes:

- defining, reviewing and reporting performance against service commitments that are recorded in customer and service provider approved Service Level Agreements
- implementing and managing service continuity arrangements
- monitoring and analysing service availability performance, and refining associated plans
- developing a service delivery budget, and managing costs against the budget
- monitoring and analysing service capacity performance, and refining associated plans
- establishing a security policy, understanding security risks, implementing security controls and managing security related incidents.

Relationship processes (Clause 7) includes:

- developing a good relationship with customers, understanding their needs and assessing customer satisfaction
- defining the scope of work for suppliers, agreeing contractual elements such as service performance targets, and the review of the success of the relationship.

Resolution processes (Clause 8) includes:

- dealing with current or potential service failures and managing service requests (e.g. extension of service hours)
- dealing with recurrent issues and preventing or mitigating them.

1: Background

Control processes (Clause 9) includes:

- managing changes to the services and supporting elements
- maintaining a current reference of service components for use by all other processes.
- establishing a test environment to validate service changes before being deployed into an operational environment
- developing and maintaining plans stating release content and release schedules.

Functional organisation structures are necessary when implementing processes, but they can lead to fostering a silo-based mentality. This risk can be mitigated through a number of approaches that will be highly dependent upon the culture of the service provider, the attitude of the staff, and their behaviours. Examples of a few effective approaches to influence the take-up of change are provided below for consideration.

- Develop and communicate an end-to-end integrated management system model, and use it to explain how individuals' roles contribute to the overall performance.
- Use key performance indicators (KPIs) that encourage measurement across the functional boundaries.
- Acknowledge behaviours that support and promote integration.
- Understand the underlying reasons why silo-based mentalities already exist, and apply appropriate methods to address these.

In summary, developing and communicating a holistic management system model will lead to more efficient and effective service delivery which, in turn, will foster a team spirit.

Focus on continual improvement

The business world never stays still. Customers' needs change and governments change laws. Global events, such as the on-going economic crisis, can have a far-reaching impact on

1: Background

organisational performance and needs. Organisations therefore seek to develop new services and products, and refine existing ones.

It is imperative that service providers are able to react to (and, where possible, predict) these changing situations, in order to respond to them. An agile service provider will reap major benefits.

The Deming cycle, referred to in clause 4.5 of the standard, provides a structured approach to contribute to an improvement in alignment to the organisation and service provider's needs. By making these improvements, and ensuring that the overall management system aligns to ISO/IEC 20000, progress can be made without slipping back (*see Figure 4*).

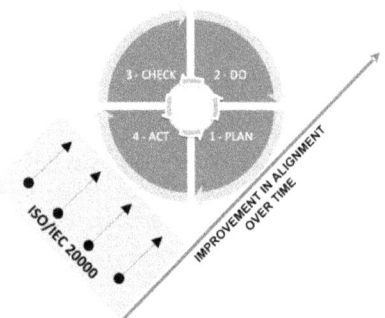

Figure 4: Plan, Do, Check and Act (PDCA) supported by ISO/IEC 20000

The outer circle shows the direction of improvement over time while aligning to the needs of the customers and of the service provider. It shows the rotational direction of the improvement, i.e. in a positive direction with the standard underpinning these improvements.

The inner circle, or the axle, shows the direction of the PDCA Deming stages.

1: Background

The **Plan** stage (Step 1) is concerned with identifying the objectives and processes required, to deliver services aligned to the organisation's needs and the service provider's policies.

The **Do** stage (Step 2) is concerned with implementing the plans in a structured way.

The **Check** stage (Step 3) is concerned with measuring and checking that the processes and services have actually achieved what they set out to achieve.

The **Act** stage (Step 4) is concerned with taking steps to improve the performance of processes.

The process of PDCA should be used, not only when setting up a service management system, but also when refining it.

In summary, by taking this approach, the integrity of the end-to-end integrated service management model can be maintained.

CHAPTER 2: KEY STAKEHOLDER BODIES

There are several key stakeholder bodies operating within the arena of the service provider. It is important to ensure that their needs are understood, and that the relationships are clearly defined and actively managed. This chapter highlights the key elements of this philosophy.

Customers and end-users

The people who receive the services and use them in order to derive value from a business perspective are the end-users. They provide input to the customers who specify the service requirements and, where applicable, pay for the services.

The customers and end-users may be internal or external to the service provider's organisation, or a combination of both.

Service providers

Types of service provider

There are two primary types of service provider, the internal service provider (ISP) and the external service provider (ESP). The ISP resides within the same organisation as the customer, while the ESP resides outside the customer's organisation and is often known as a 'managed service provider'.

While the core service management system activities remain the same between the two types, there can be a different emphasis placed on various service management elements. For example, an ESP would typically have more emphasis on cross-selling services in order to leverage additional value from the commercial contract with the customer.

It is the service provider who would seek certification or compliance with ISO/IEC 20000.

2: Key Stakeholder Bodies

If certification is the target, the service provider must be able to present sufficient evidence to satisfy a certification body auditor that they are conforming to the standard, in order for them to achieve certification. Fundamentally, the service provider will also need to carry on doing the good work that they started, as the auditors will return to check this on an annual basis. There should, therefore, be an emphasis on retaining certification from the outset.

It is not enough for the service provider to simply provide access to its process/procedure definitions, policies and plans. They also need to provide evidence of how these have been used to support the commitments made. Additionally, a track record needs to be in place demonstrating that they have performed to their defined management system and the requirements of the standard for an absolute minimum period of three months. Typically, though, a twelve-month period, or longer, is required.

Service management staff

The importance of the contribution of service management staff to the overall success of the service management organisation should not be underestimated. These are the people who manage services through the service life cycle and design, implement and maintain the management system, perhaps with external consultancy or interim resource support.

It will be no surprise, then, that compliance and certification to ISO/IEC 20000 can only be achieved by the service provider having competent service management staff in place.

Reassuringly, the standard recognises the role that these people play. There is a whole clause dedicated to the requirements on a service provider for addressing the competence, awareness and training of these individuals while also checking the effectiveness of actions taken to support the them.

As experienced change practitioners will know, defining processes is one thing, implementing them, and ensuring that people are embracing the changes is another. The journey should always begin with this challenge in mind. Mitigating actions should be put in place throughout the stages of change. These could include actions such as those below.

- Identifying and involving key stakeholders as early in the life cycle as possible.
- Providing access to a model office environment to showcase (and validate) the new ways of working.
- Tailoring training that embraces any adopted framework (best practice) and the service provider's own management system.
- Employing a disciplined approach to fulfilling commitments. One of the biggest demotivators is the lack of follow-through.
- Addressing issues that can be predicted, rather than avoiding them and hoping that they will go away. This can be achieved through open communication and a genuine interest in gaining feedback from those affected, then doing something with it.

Internal auditors

Service providers should take full ownership and accountability for their performance. An integral part of this consists in ongoing and regular planned internal auditing via competent auditors.

This role may be performed via various routes.

- Larger service providers may have a dedicated internal audit function.
- Others may integrate it into an existing role, often that of the service level manager, as they are normally responsible for providing a view of the overall service quality to the customer.
- It is also an option to outsource this activity to competent and experienced external consultants who may have a wider industry view. However, 'process governance' must be retained by the service provider. The concept of

2: Key Stakeholder Bodies

process governance is explained in the next section of this book and in detail in Part 3 of ISO/IEC 20000.

Whichever route the service provider chooses, it is imperative that the auditor remains independent of the documents and records that they are auditing. They cannot audit their own work.

ISO/IEC 20000 provides a series of requirements related to the audit capability in Clause 4.5.4, Monitor and review the SMS (Check) (Step 3) of the PDCA cycle.

Suppliers

Service providers often rely upon the expertise of external suppliers. Critically, when any aspect of service provision is outsourced, it is the service provider who must 'retain process governance' of the activities. This is qualified as follows, in that the service provider must:

- have defined key performance indicators with targets that are checked and actioned to ensure alignment to the performance characteristics (the **M**ETRICS)
- ensure that they are accountable for process operation, irrespective of which part of the supply chain is operating the processes (retaining **A**CCOUNTABILITY)
- perform activities to improve the management system and service provided within the constraints of the service provider (implementing **I**MPROVEMENTS)
- control the definition of the processes and their interfaces (control the **D**EFINITION).

A good memory jogger for these four elements is **MAID**: **M**etrics, **A**ccountability, **I**mprovements and **D**efinition of processes.

ISO/IEC 20000 uses specific terminology when referring to suppliers. *Suppliers* and *lead suppliers* have a direct relationship with the service provider. *Subcontracted suppliers* have a direct relationship with *lead suppliers*, as shown in Figure 5.

2: Key Stakeholder Bodies

It is the responsibility of the service provider to ensure that the direct relationships are clearly defined, formalised in an agreement, and managed. They should also ensure that any subcontracted work aligns to the requirements specified by the service provider.

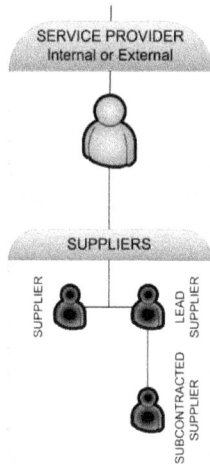

Figure 5: The supply chain

Suppliers do not need to have ISO/IEC 20000 certification in order for a service provider to achieve certification. In practice, however, it can make the service provider's life easier if they do.

Certification bodies

This stakeholder is responsible for a third-party audit of the service provider's management system. They are external auditors.

Following a successful initial audit, a *certification audit*, the certification body will award the ISO/IEC 20000 certificate, and license the use of any related logo to the service provider.

2: Key Stakeholder Bodies

This audit is performed against the Part 1 requirements, and is conducted initially and on every third anniversary of the initial award of the certificate.

Of course, the service provider needs to continue to perform during the interim period between the certification audits. An annual 'surveillance audit' is therefore carried out by the certification body, concentrating on previous areas of concern and a snapshot of the standard.

With both types of audit, a track record is explored to ensure that the service provider is doing what they intended to do, in a consistent and repeatable way.

The certification body is accredited initially by their National Accreditation Body (NAB). The following list represents those NABs in countries where ISO/IEC 20000 is particularly popular.

- American National Standards Institute (ANAB).
- China National Accreditation Service (CNAS) for conformity assessment.
- Japan Accreditation Board (JAB) for conformity assessment.
- Korea Accreditation Board (KAB).
- National Accreditation Board for Certification Bodies (NABCB) India.
- United Kingdom Accreditation Service (UKAS).

They are all members of the International Accreditation Forum (IAF) which provides a level of international governance of certification bodies, ensuring only competent bodies are accredited.

For a full list of IAF NABs visit *www.iaf.nu*.

The certification bodies follow strict rules when auditing management systems. In fact, the standard, ISO/IEC 17021, is used as a global focal point. It contains principles and requirements for the competence, consistency and impartiality of the audit and certification of management systems of all

2: Key Stakeholder Bodies

types (e.g. quality management systems or environmental management systems) and for bodies providing these activities.

A list of accredited certification bodies under the APMG International certification scheme for service providers can be found at *http://www.isoiec20000certification.com/home/CertificationBodies/RCBs/RCBsListings.aspx*.

Enabling bodies

Accredited Training Providers (ATPs)

ATPs can play a vital role in helping service provider staff, in particular, to understand what is required to design, implement and operate a service management system that could ultimately lead to ISO/IEC 20000 certification and retention where required.

The training providers are accredited by their chosen exam institute. The links below provide access to the current list of accredited training providers for those institutes referred to in this book.

- APMGI-accredited course providers

    http://www.apmg-international.com/home/Qualifications/ISOIEC20000Quals.asp

- BCS-accredited training providers

    http://www.bcs.org/category/9801

- EXIN-accredited training providers

    http://www.exin.com/NL/en/exams/find-trainer?&target=company

2: Key Stakeholder Bodies

Consultants

Starting on the road to designing, implementing and operating an effective and efficient service management system can be quite daunting. That is why an ISO/IEC 20000 lead approach, complemented by the service provider's framework of choice, can simplify the process. It can still prove difficult to overcome the inertia from time to time, which is where external expertise can really make the difference.

When choosing consultants to assist with a service management improvement initiative using this approach, there are many considerations to take into account. A checklist could include the questions below.

- Do they have specific experience of service management within an ISO/IEC 20000 context?
- What is their approach to enabling cultural change?
- Do they understand the process of certification?
- Do they understand how related standards integrate with ISO/IEC 20000?
- Is their pedigree in this field recognised within the service management industry?

Guidance for consultants and service providers can be found in the itSMF International endorsed publication, *Implementing ISO/IEC 20000 – The Roadmap*, author – David Clifford, enterprise-DNA Limited.

CHAPTER 3: QUALIFICATION PROGRAMMES

A number of examination institutes have recognised the ever-growing importance and position of ISO/IEC 20000 within the market place. As a result, new qualifications aligned to the standard have emerged. This chapter provides an overview of the prime movers in this field.

Positioning of the EXIN ITSM qualifications

EXIN have developed a new ITSM qualification programme, as shown in the figure on the next page.

They have taken a very different approach when designing their service management qualification programme. They have used ISO/IEC 20000 as a vehicle to define the boundaries of the syllabuses. As discussed earlier, the philosophy of 'concentrate on what you must do, as opposed to everything that you could do' is a sound one. This philosophy has been reflected in the qualification programme design. Additionally, a role-based approach has been used to ensure that the qualifications at the various levels fit the needs of the roles.

3: Qualification Programmes

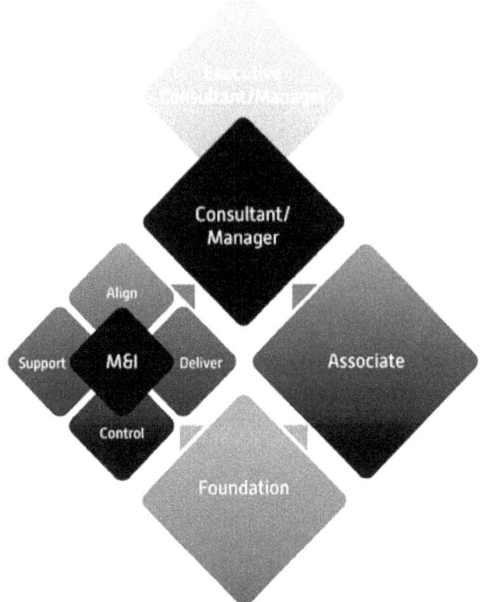

Figure 6: Structure of the EXIN ITSM qualification programme

This has led to a number of benefits:

- course attendees will be able to focus on the critical activities, as opposed to having a superficial understanding across a wider array of activities
- a more practical emphasis on 'how to' can be used, thereby giving an increased probability that the attendees can practise what they have learnt when they return to their roles
- training can explore the depths of service management activities to a greater degree

3: Qualification Programmes

- through the alignment to ISO/IEC 20000, the brand is strong and well known worldwide, benefiting the recognition of the attendees
- training time can be reduced and therefore money can be saved.

EXIN have also provided a facility to recognise existing investment in training through the recognition of other qualification schemes via side-entry routes. This enables a complementary approach to be taken.

In summary, they have taken a 'lean' style approach to their qualification programme, ensuring that a practical and pragmatic focus on service management is employed.

The following paragraphs provide an insight into the syllabuses of the various qualifications. This is not intended to provide a complete list of exam specifications. For full details, visit *www.exin-ITSM.com*.

Foundation level – main points

IS20F *Foundation*

- Typical course duration – 15 hours (2 days).
- Exam – 40 multiple choice questions, 1 hour. 26 correct answers needed for a pass.
- Understanding the definitions and principles of service quality management.
- Understanding the position of ISO/IEC 20000 in service management.
- The quality specifications for service management.

Recognition

- The qualification provides a credit in the ITIL® qualification scheme.
- It also provides 1 point when applying to become a credential holder in The priSM Institute® and 6 continual professional development credits.

3: Qualification Programmes

IS20FB *Foundation Bridge*

- Typical course duration – 6½ hours (1 day).
- Exam – 20 multiple choice questions, 30 minutes. 13 correct answers needed for a pass.
- Understanding a quality approach to service management.
- Understanding the landscapes of standards and frameworks.
- Understanding the concepts of certification practices.

Professional level – main points

All exams at the professional level have the same format and the courses have the same duration.

- Typical course duration – 18 hours (3 days, although two modules can be combined into a 5-day session, for economy of scale).
- Exam – 40 multiple choice scenario questions, 90 minutes. 26 correct answers needed for a pass.

Recognition

- The professional level qualifications provide 2 points when applying to become a credential holder in The priSM Institute® and 12 continual professional development credits for IS20PMI/IS20ACA and 6 continual professional development credits for all others.

IS20PMI *Management and Improvement of Service Management Processes*

- Align service management to changes in the business.
- Maintain the management system.
- Apply the continual service improvement life cycle.
- Analyse compliance and efficiency.
- *Scope of processes* – requirements for a management system, and planning and implementing service management.

3: Qualification Programmes

IS20PA *Alignment of Service Management and the Business*

- Plan the processes for the alignment of service management and the business.
- Implement and manage the alignment of service management and the business.
- Measure, monitor and report on the alignment of service management and the business.
- Improve the alignment of service management and the business.
- *Scope of processes* – business relationship management, supplier management, service level management, service reporting, and budgeting and accounting.

IS20PC *Control of Services*

- Plan the processes for control of the services.
- Implement and manage the processes for control of the services.
- Measure, monitor and report on the processes for control of the services.
- Improve the processes for control of the services.
- *Scope of processes* – planning and implementing new or changed services, configuration management, change management and release management.

The IS20PS *Support of Services*

- Plan the processes for support of the services.
- Implement and manage the processes for support of the services.
- Measure, monitor and report on the processes for support of the services.
- Improve the processes for support of the services.
- *Scope of processes* – incident and problem management.

IS20PD *Delivery of Services*

- Plan the processes for delivery of the services.

- Implement and manage the processes for delivery of the services.
- Measure, monitor and report on the processes for delivery of the services.
- Improve the processes for delivery of the services.
- *Scope of processes* – service continuity management, availability management, capacity management and information security management.

IS20ACA *Associate Consultant/Auditor*

- Typical course duration – 36 hours (5 days).
- Exam – 80 multiple choice scenario questions, 120 minutes. 52 correct answers needed for a pass.
- A cut across all of the professional level modules with a particular emphasis on the 'management and improvement of service management' processes.

Management track

IS20CM *Consultant/Manager in ITSM*

- Typical course duration – 21 hours (3 days).
- Exam – 20 multiple choice/multiple response questions plus 3 essay questions, 120 minutes. A score of 50% or more in each paper, and a combined score of 65% or more is needed for a pass.
- Establishing the service management plan.
- Motivating people.
- Assessing and reporting on the service management system.
- Managing service improvements.

IS20ECM *Executive Consultant/Manager in ITSM*

- Typical course duration – 2 days for Session 1 followed by a 3-month practical project period, then 2 days for Session 2.

3: Qualification Programmes

- Assessment is conducted via a combination of methods including assessment of:
  - knowledge and experience prior to entry to the module
  - sharing of existing knowledge through a presentation and a question and answer session
  - development of a paper based upon a practical project regarding the application of service management in the workplace – duration 3 months
  - presentation of the journey taken during the project.
- Setting the direction for service management.
- Directing the service management function.
- Monitoring the performance of service management.
- Governing the service management system.

BCS qualification

BCS introduced a single qualification at the foundation level for ISO/IEC 20000.

The following paragraphs provide an insight into the syllabus of the qualification. This is not intended to provide a complete list of exam specifications. For full details, visit *http://www.bcs.org/category/9794.*

Foundation level

BCS *Foundation*

- Typical course duration – 18 hours (3 days).
- Exam – 40 multiple choice questions, 1 hour. 26 correct answers required to pass.
- Understanding ISO/IEC 20000 scope, purpose and use.

3: Qualification Programmes

- Understanding an integrated approach to maintaining an IT service management system.
- Describe the scope and eligibility requirements and options to achieve certification.
- Understand and describe the PDCA cycle.
- Understand the requirements of ISO/IEC 20000
- Explain how assessments, reviews and internal audits are used.

APMGI qualifications

APMG-International™
ISO/IEC 20000

The following paragraphs provide an insight into the syllabuses of the three qualifications that APMGI have in this field. This is not intended to provide a complete list of exam specifications.

For details of the qualification scheme visit *http://www.apmg-international.com/home/Qualifications/ISOIEC20000Quals.asp.*

APMGI *Foundation*

- Typical course duration – 3 days.
- Exam – 40 multiple choice questions, 1 hour. 26 correct answers required to pass.
- The background to the ISO/IEC 20000 standard and the associated APMG-International certification and qualification schemes.
- The scope and purpose of ISO/IEC 20000-1 (Specification), ISO/IEC 20000-2 (Code of Practice) and ISO/IEC 20000-3 (Guidance on Scope and Applicability of ISO/IEC 20000-1) and how these can be used.

3: Qualification Programmes

- The terms, definitions and requirements contained in ISO/IEC 20000-1.
- The fundamental requirements for an IT Service Management System and the need for continual improvement.
- Eligibility, scoping requirements and the role of process owners and practitioners in the preparation for ISO/IEC 20000 certification.
- Assessments, informal and RCB audits, and the associated terminology.

Recognition

- The qualification provides 1 credit in the ITIL® qualification scheme.

APMGI *Auditor*

- Typical course duration – 2 days.
- Exam – 25 multiple choice questions, 1 hour. 18 correct answers required to pass.
- The contents, requirements, objectives and application of ISO/IEC 20000-1:2005 (Specification).
- IT Service Management Principles.
- How to resolve ITSM Service Provider's eligibility and scoping issues.
- Application and relevance of ISO/IEC 20000-2:2005 (Code of Practice) to audits.
- What is required in pre-audits and formal certification and surveillance audits.

Recognition

- The qualification provides 1 credit in the ITIL® qualification scheme.
- It also provides 2 points when applying to become a credential holder in The priSM Institute® and 12 continual professional development credits.

3: Qualification Programmes

APMGI *Practitioner*

- Typical course duration – 3 days.
- Exam – 25 multiple choice questions, 1 hour, plus a written paper, 1 hour. A score of 50% or more in each paper, plus a combined score of 65% or more, is required to pass.
- Understand the relationship between the ISO/IEC 20000 standard and IT Service Management.
- Assist in ISO/IEC 200000 certification readiness assessments and certification audits.
- Understand and explain the potential issues regarding applicability, eligibility and scoping.
- Produce a gap analysis supported by an improvement and implementation plan.
- Assist and advise organisations regarding implementation of continual improvement processes.
- Help organisations achieve ISO/IEC 20000 certification.

Recognition

- The qualification provides 1.5 credits in the ITIL® qualification scheme.
- It also provides 2 points when applying to become a credential holder in The priSM Institute® and 12 continual professional development credits.

CHAPTER 4: COMPLIANCE AND CERTIFICATION

What is compliance?

Compliance is the ability to demonstrate internal conformity and adherence to service provider policies, plans, procedures, regulations, contracts, and the requirements of ISO/IEC 20000. This would be validated via a *first-party audit*.

What is due diligence?

Due diligence is where a customer performs an assessment of a service provider's status, prior to engaging them to perform activities on the customer's behalf. This could include, but may not be limited to:

- financial status
- legal position
- standing in the industry
- stability
- approach to innovation and risk.

Due diligence can also fall within a general *second-party audit* strategy, where the customer's organisation performs an audit on the service provider.

Certification to ISO/IEC 20000 will provide the potential customer's organisation with a level of comfort regarding the service provider's service management capability. This is why more and more service providers are being required to become certified to the standard. For example, the US Federal Government has specified this for their service providers for particular types of contract award.

Nonetheless, certification to ISO/IEC 20000 should not preclude customers from performing additional due diligence checks.

4: Compliance and Certification

What is certification?

It is where an independent *third-party audit* has been performed by a certification body, and they have confirmed that the service provider is conformant to the requirements of the standard. Certification is awarded against the management system itself, as opposed to the services or products being offered.

Why certify?

Although benefit can be derived from simply using the standard as a simple checklist of activities that need to be performed, i.e. compliance, further benefits can be derived from formal certification.

- It demonstrates confidence that the service provider can carry on performing well.
- It can allow service providers to bid for new work.
- It gives the service provider's staff formal external recognition that they are working together as a team and are considering the customer.
- It can be used as a marketing vehicle to show potential external customers that the service provider knows how to manage a service management capability.
- It can help internal service providers to demonstrate the value that they add to the organisation.
- It can assist in maintaining focus for ongoing conformity to the standard and the service provider's own policies, processes and procedures.

What is the auditor's approach?

The auditor will take a positive approach to the process. However, they will require to see evidence that the requirements of the standard have been satisfied consistently over a period of time.

4: Compliance and Certification

When validating the service provider's capability using Part 1 of ISO/IEC 20000, the auditor will check that evidence is:

- **d**ocumented – a formal definition of the artefact is made
- **c**ommunicated – people understand what is being discussed
- **u**sed – a formal record of activity against the stated intentions is made
- **r**eviewed – to check that activities are still fit for purpose
- **i**mproved – to check that progress is being made on non-conformities.

This is known as the **DCURI** cycle.

The auditor may rate each of their assessments as non-conformant (major or minor) or conformant (perhaps with an observation).

Certification to ISO/IEC 20000 will be withheld if there are any assessments that indicate that there is a fundamental breakdown of the management system.

CHAPTER 5: CERTIFICATION SCHEMES

The APMGI certification scheme

Certification schemes enable service providers to become certified to the standard. They effectively allow a service management team to be recognised as working well together based upon the requirements of the standard. Certification schemes should not be confused with qualification schemes or programmes. Certification schemes in this context are for service provider entities, while qualification schemes or programmes are for individuals.

The scheme which APMGI launched operates on a global basis. They register certification bodies so that these Registered Certification Bodies (RCBs) can perform audits to the additional audit rules identified by APMGI. These are documented and freely available at :

http://www.isoiec20000certification.com/home/certificationbodies/RCBs.aspx

It is a requirement that RCBs are already accredited by their National Accreditation Body (NAB) to perform management system audits.

The APMGI certification scheme dictates that all requirements within the standard must be satisfied in order for a certificate to be awarded.

Other certification schemes

There is nothing to preclude any organisation from establishing its own certification scheme based on its own rules. ISO/IEC do not have any direct involvement in the management or approval of certification schemes.

5: Certification Schemes

APMGI operates one such scheme, and there are others around the globe, such as the BSI Management Systems scheme, and the Japan Quality Assurance organisation scheme.

Note

The rules that are given to the certification bodies to use when auditing can differ between certification scheme owners. Therefore, any entity that is looking at an ISO/IEC 20000 certified service provider should validate which certification scheme it was awarded under, and the terms of auditing that were used, particularly whether all, or a sub-set, of ISO/IEC 20000 requirements were assessed.

How many certificates have been awarded?

It is currently impossible to state the precise number of certificates awarded, and to whom, as some certification scheme owners publish this information and others do not. APMGI does publish its information, to be found on the *www.isoiec20000certification.com* website.

When considering all certification schemes, it is believed that a few thousand certificates have been awarded around the world.

Another way to look at the popularity of the standard is to look at the number of sales of ISO/IEC 20000 when compared to other standards from the same field. This standard significantly outsells the others.

CHAPTER 6: SCOPE OF ASSESSMENT

Defining a scope statement

The most common area for debate and confusion is that of defining an appropriate scope for assessment against ISO/IEC 20000. This is primarily due to the fact that there are many potential options for a service provider.

Fundamentally, before setting off down a route to compliance and, perhaps, certification to the standard, service providers should understand what they are trying to achieve, and why.

For some service providers, the definition of scope may be predefined, as their customers have specified that they need to achieve certification for a particular contract.

> For example, BT Global Services were successful with bids for services to the UK's National Health Service (NHS), the customer. As part of the overall change programme, the NHS specified that all its direct service providers must become certified to ISO/IEC 20000 for the services provided to it within a specific period of time. External service providers are quite often dictated to, in terms of the scope of certification.

A service provider may also elect themselves to be assessed against the standard, perhaps to assist in driving through improvements in their management system.

What is it that is being assessed?

It is important to recall that the focus for auditing against ISO/IEC 20000 is on the service management system. This includes the policies, processes, plans and support mechanisms that enable products or services to be delivered.

6: Scope of Assessment

In order to validate that the management system is performing to the requirements of ISO/IEC 20000, *test data* needs to be used.

> A good analogy is a Formula One car. It goes through design, build and wind tunnel testing stages to prepare it for service based on the agreed specifications. By the end of this process, the latent capability, the *management system* is in existence.
>
> To validate that it performs to specification, the car needs to be used on various circuits around the world. So, in this case, the test data would be the different circuit characteristics, with associated documentation and records of activities.

Following through on the NHS example, BT Global Services defined the following scope statement:

> The provision of IT service management activities related to the NHS N3 service, NHS National Spine service and NHS London cluster.

Here, therefore, the IT service management activities were audited using test data supporting the NHS N3, Spine and London cluster services. The test data would have been limited to those documents and records particular to the specified services.

What are the parameters for scope statements?

There are four primary parameters used to define the scope of auditing, but others can apply (*see Figure 7*).

A scope statement can be defined using the following template:

> The service management system of the **service provider** that delivers **services** to **customer(s)** from **location(s)**.

The parameters enable a service provider to limit the scope to a subset of their service provision, or to encapsulate the whole service offering, depending on the drivers for assessment to the standard.

6: Scope of Assessment

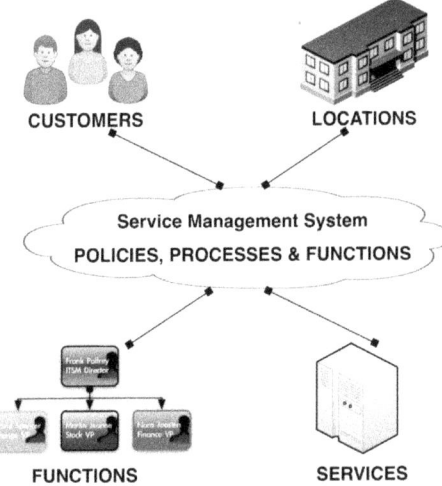

Figure 7: Scope parameters

For example, a global service provider, Joosten BV, could specify that they wish to learn from an initial foray into standards certification, and limit the scope to the internal services offered from their western European base in Delft, the Netherlands.

A scope statement for this example would be:

> The service management system of **Joosten BV** that delivers all **services** to its **internal customers** from **Delft, The Netherlands**.

It should be clearly noted that standards certification is predicated on the principle of assessing the management system against all of the requirements of the standard. Therefore, when scope is discussed in this context, it only applies to the test data used to validate that the management system is functioning in accordance with the requirements of the standard. In this case, certification may only be awarded to

6: Scope of Assessment

a single legal entity, the service provider which is able to demonstrate conformance to all of the requirements.

Part 3 of ISO/IEC 20000 provides many examples of scope statements and further information regarding auditing.

The role of existing certifications

In practice, service providers may already have certification to other standards, typically, the ISO/IEC 27001 standard for Information Security Management, or the ISO9001 Standard for Quality Management Systems.

Service providers who have a valid current certificate for one of these two standards will find it easier to demonstrate conformance to some of the requirements of ISO/IEC 20000.

For example, the information security management requirements in Clause 6.6 of ISO/IEC 20000 will be satisfied by a service provider who has certification for ISO/IEC 27001, as long as the scope is complementary. ISO9001 has strong links with Clause 4 (service management system general requirements) of ISO/IEC 20000.

CHAPTER 7: RELATIONSHIP WITH OTHER STANDARDS

ISO/IEC 27001

The ISO/IEC 27000 family of standards is focused on Information Security Management Systems (ISMS). ISO/IEC 27001 specifies the requirements that service providers shall follow. It includes, but is not limited to, the definition and management of risks and controls pertinent to the information security policy. The standard embraces those critical elements identified in Section 6.6 'Information Security Management' of ISO/IEC 20000, but also goes much further in its requirements for information security management systems.

ISO/IEC 15504

This standard provides guidance on process assessment, and specific models for particular arenas. It will help to drive out process improvement. Part 8, specific to service management, is currently being developed (*see Chapter 8 for further details*).

ISO9001

The ISO9000 family of standards is focused on quality management systems at an enterprise level. In summary, it requires that procedures are formally documented, that processes are monitored to ensure they remain effective over time, that records of activities are maintained, that formal corrective action is employed where necessary, and that continual improvement is evidenced. It is not specific to the operation of a service management service provider – it remains generic. Organisations seeking to validate that their service management system is operating to a defined level should consider referring to ISO/IEC 20000.

7: Relationship with other Standards

Integrated management systems

PAS 99 is a Publicly Available Specification, published by the BSI, of interest to service providers who wish to integrate its management systems. It addresses the following standards by providing a cross reference of requirements:

- **ISO9001** – quality
- **ISO14001** – environment
- **BS OHSAS 18001** – occupational health & safety
- **ISO/IEC 20000** – service management
- **ISO22000** – food safety
- **ISO/IEC 27001** – information security management.

By taking an integrated management system approach, some of the following benefits may be realised:

- reduced cost through efficiency savings
- reduced time through effectiveness savings
- cross-discipline integration, leading to closer working between the teams
- improved core business focus
- reduced audit effort through consolidated audits.

CHAPTER 8: THE FUTURE OF ISO/IEC 20000

Overview of the parts of ISO/IEC 20000

The following section provides a catalogue of the different parts of ISO/IEC 20000 together with predictions of when the various new parts/editions of ISO/IEC 20000 will be released. It is impossible to be specific on this, as there are many key stakeholders in the process of developing standards who have to be consulted before publication.

ISO/IEC 20000 Part 1: Edition 2 "Service management system requirements"

- Launched 15th April 2011.
- Provides the specifications (requirements) for IT service management systems.

ISO/IEC 20000 Part 2: Edition 2 "Guidance on the application of service management systems"

- Expected publication by end of Q1-2012.
- It is being updated to re-align with Edition 2 of ISO/IEC 20000 Part 1.

ISO/IEC 20000 Part 3: Edition 2 "Guidance on scope definition and applicability of ISO/IEC 20000 Part 1"

- Expected publication to be confirmed.
- Provides guidance on the scope and applicability of ISO/IEC 20000. Being revised to align to the new edition of Part 1 and to convert it to a standard (from a technical report).

ISO/IEC 20000 Part 4: Edition 1 "Process reference model"

- Launched 25th November 2010.

8: The Future of ISO/IEC 20000

- A process reference model (PRM) is a logical representation of the elements of the processes within service management that can be performed at a basic level. Each process of this process reference model is described in terms of a purpose and outcomes.

ISO/IEC 20000 Part 5: Edition 1 "Exemplar implementation plan for ISO/IEC 20000 Part 1"

- Launched 26th April 2010.
- An exemplar implementation plan providing guidance to service providers on how to implement a service management system to fulfil the requirements of ISO/IEC 20000-1 or for service providers who are planning service improvements and intending to use ISO/IEC 20000 as a business goal.

For the latest updates on ISO/IEC 20000 developments visit:
http://enterprise-dna.com/enterprise-DNA/info-PORTAL_-_ISO_IEC_20000.html

ABBREVIATIONS USED

APMGI	APMG International
BCS	The Chartered Institute for IT
BSI	British Standards Institute
CNAS	China National Accreditation Service
COBIT	Control Objectives for Information and related Technology; a set of best practices (framework) for information technology (IT) management
DCURI	Documented, Communicated, Used, Reviewed, Improved
ESP	External Service Provider
eTom	Enhanced Telecom Operations Map, now the Business Process Framework
EXIN	Examination Institute for Information Science
IAF	International Accreditation Forum
IEC	International Electrotechnical Commission
ISMS	Information Security Management Systems
ISO	International Organisation for Standardisation
ISP	Internal Service Provider
ITIL	The Information Technology Infrastructure Library, a set of concepts and practices for managing ITSM
itSMF	IT Service Management Forum
ITSM	IT Service Management
JAB	Japan Accreditation Board

Abbreviations Used

MAID	Metrics, Accountability, Improvements and Definition of processes
MOF	Microsoft Operations Framework; practical guidance for everyday IT practices and activities
NAB	National Accreditation Body
NABCB	National Accreditation Board for Certification Bodies
NHS	National Health Service
PAM	Process Assessment Model
PDCA	Plan, Do, Check, Act
PRISM	Professional Recognition of Individuals in Service Management (*www.theprisminstitute.org*)
PRM	Process Reference Model
RCB	Registered Certification Body
SMS	Service Management System

ITG RESOURCES

IT Governance Ltd. sources, creates and delivers products and services to meet the real-world, evolving IT governance needs of today's organisations, directors, managers and practitioners.

The ITG website (*www.itgovernance.co.uk*) is the international one-stop-shop for corporate and IT governance information, advice, guidance, books, tools, training and consultancy.

www.itgovernance.co.uk/iso20000.aspx is the section of our website for ISO20000 resources.

Other Websites

Books and tools published by IT Governance Publishing (ITGP) are available from all business booksellers and are also immediately available from the following websites:

www.itgovernance.co.uk/catalog/355 provides information and online purchasing facilities for every currently available book published by ITGP.

www.itgovernance.eu is our euro-denominated website which ships from Benelux and has a growing range of books in European languages other than English.

www.itgovernanceusa.com is a US$-based website that delivers the full range of IT Governance products to North America, and ships from within the continental US.

www.itgovernanceasia.com provides a selected range of ITGP products specifically for customers in South Asia.

www.27001.com is the IT Governance Ltd. website that deals specifically with information security management, and ships from within the continental US.

Pocket Guides

For full details of the entire range of pocket guides, simply follow the links at *www.itgovernance.co.uk/publishing.aspx*.

ITG Resources

Toolkits

ITG's unique range of toolkits includes the IT Governance Framework Toolkit, which contains all the tools and guidance that you will need in order to develop and implement an appropriate IT governance framework for your organisation. Full details can be found at *www.itgovernance.co.uk/products/519*.

For a free paper on how to use the proprietary Calder-Moir IT Governance Framework, and for a free trial version of the toolkit, see *www.itgovernance.co.uk/calder_moir.aspx*.

There is also a wide range of toolkits to simplify implementation of management systems, such as an ISO/IEC 27001 ISMS or a BS25999 BCMS, and these can all be viewed and purchased online at *www.itgovernance.co.uk/catalog/1*.

Best Practice Reports

ITG's range of Best Practice Reports is now at *www.itgovernance.co.uk/best-practice-reports.aspx*. These offer you essential, pertinent, expertly researched information on a number of key issues including Web 2.0 and Green IT.

Training and Consultancy

IT Governance also offers training and consultancy services across the entire spectrum of disciplines in the information governance arena. Details of training courses can be accessed at *www.itgovernance.co.uk/training.aspx* and descriptions of our consultancy services can be found at *www.itgovernance.co.uk/consulting.aspx*.
Why not contact us to see how we could help you and your organisation?

Newsletter

IT governance is one of the hottest topics in business today, not least because it is also the fastest moving, so what better way to keep up than by subscribing to ITG's free monthly newsletter, *Sentinel*? It provides monthly updates and resources across the whole spectrum of IT governance subject matter, including risk management, information security, ITIL and IT service

ITG Resources

management, project governance, compliance and so much more. Subscribe for your free copy at *www.itgovernance.co.uk/newsletter.aspx*.

Lightning Source UK Ltd.
Milton Keynes UK
UKHW010950080223
416610UK00015B/1850